SEASONS OF UNKNOWN

Seasons of Unknown

Rachel Michelle Bednarz

Middle Ground Press

ISBN: 9798998761157

Book cover art by John Bednarz

First Printing, 2025

To anyone walking into their unknown.

CONTENTS

INTRODUCTION

When you graduate college and move to a new city, it feels like you have woken from someone else's dream.

Why do my holidays feel different? Where did that last feeling go? Am I grown now? Why does my life still feel unknown?

These are the questions that plague the mind of a girl in her mid-twenties. She achieved some of her wildest dreams, yet she still wonders what is to come.

This is that story. A collection of recollections, feelings and sticky thoughts that cling to her mind through the night and deep into the repetitive morning.

Through it all, the post-developmental tribulations, she recognizes one thing to stand true:

Your seasons will never be the same.

The season you are in will come to pass. Once gone you will not be able to recall those philosophic thoughts and feelings which brought you through. They melt away with your perception of reality in a season new.

Perhaps each season is of itself, unknown, and to feel known is but an opportunity to renew.

This is a journey to discover if what you knew last season is worth knowing at all. Learning and relearning day in and day out. If only to understand that today's knowledge is only for just that, today.

There is a part of me
that felt inadequate
Uncool
Dull

She sulked and brooded
Caught in the me-ness of it all

Then she woke up at 23
Noticed the world around

The world she inhabits
The uniquely personal
Independently abundant
Undoubtedly her own of it all

For all she has known
and all she ever will

Fall

It was a Friday
when we moved
A new and vibrant city

We rushed and ran with excitement
Wore ourselves to bones
for two days straight
Until Sunday evening sang her song
of familiarity and order

Through it all we were tired
My eyes glazed at this very page
My feet blistered and sore

Our sole dim lamp illuminated the corner
and there you were
Folding and sorting laundry
just as Sunday begs us to

As my eyelids grew heavy
I lay awake with you
breathed in our new air
took in our new sights

In this familiarity of you
I noticed
we are finally home

When the child asked
Mama, why is the tree sad?
Her eyes were full of youthful glow
at the ability of a figure of nature
to portray ethereal emotion
Mother's eyes glaze
reflect the emotion in herself

The child does not see
The children have grown
They moved away
Visits have grown few
with far between

The old woman
who sits in the window
admires the tree's ability
to withstand such emotion its whole life
She slumbers for longer now
their winters grow dreary now

No one can quite explain
why the tree is so sad
It has lived such full life

Best friend
I miss you
Now that we have grown
I have moved away

Remember how
just weeks ago we walked
our small town neighborhood
Retired to each other's tiny apartment homes
for chilled wine
Religious quality time

How we gossiped
and eavesdropped
for the entertainment of building some drama
a little tension
in our happy and content universe

Best friend
I miss you
With this piece of us in the distance
cemented in memory

I know your truths in my heart
Now from afar
I see you grow
You inspire me
with passion
and kindness
wherever we are

A part of me lingers
high above my head
The woman I believe I will be
The woman I believe to hold my full truth

A wild and wicked ball of curiosity
in her light and delicate hand

She presides over me
with wise willpower and determination
strengths I have yet to learn

What if
I made her no promises
Stripped her of my feeble aspirations

What if
I held her to no standards
Accepted her in the form she comes

What if
I washed her of expectations
Those I cast inward
those drawn in from the outside
the holy
the earthly
the spiritual

What will remain
in my goddess' garden
If I rip out all the stems
cast aside the stepping stones
heave the fence from its posts

let the wild things roam

When I till the tired soil
with my worn and cracked hands

What will grow
when no roots remain?

As we grow
some things remain
far past what we once thought to be
their date of expiry

I overheard the adults once
Mom and aunt brush elbows over appetizers
at family holiday

Casual conversation
adults growing older
kids overhearing

What did you think would go away
as you got older
but never did?

Pimples, anxiety, comparison...

A list I now add to
tally for myself
What I wish I had known
What I wish had gone away
The quiet pressures of school yard days

Yet
as you grow older
your peers do too

There is no ultimate villain
cowering in a dark corner
waiting for you to stumble in
offering aspirations of sin

Pressure
it is cautious to reveal itself
a slow acting venom
in the throes of daily life

Peers
Your friends
They want the best for you
but do not know the best for themselves

The waking of October
startles the mind
Year after year
the month creeps in

Fall does not snap her fingers
When you wake
she is there
She has been there
for some time now

The past you
who you ran from all summer
comes to light
in the space between branches
illuminated by the fallen leaves

Autumn slips the covers over you
at night
She cracks the window
lets herself in

October
The month, the sensation
she kisses the stretch of your skin
Reconciliation for the growing pains
of a new season

Briefly you see it
A flash of self reflection
in the trees
A shedding of who you
have known yourself to be

Your mind
your media
play clever tricks on you
They fill your shoes with guilt
weigh you down
as you trudge the path ahead

But you know the truth
of your soul
You wish the best
for all you come across

In quiet comfort
you know this to be true
of others for you

For others need not know
your greatest intention
or understand the will of your heart

You may not bow your head each evening
Prayer may not be the only outlet
for gratitude and hope to exude

You know
your heart burns big and red
a different shade
over each friend's horizon
as each of theirs' do for you

A mosaic sunset
eclipsed only in the brief doubt
of your own moon

Maybe you felt betrayed
As I felt our stitches pull away
I did not have the strength yet to mend
what it meant to be your friend
Slipped my scissors
under the unwoven thread

It was soft
and sweet
and gentle
in my head

Now I do not know
what I am supposed to feel
like you were tethered to my Achilles' heel

A tug of gravity
pulling us from the sky

I planted my feet on the ground
Squeezed the fresh grass between my toes
No words whispered
Arm up to the sky
Let you go

A balloon
released from its string
once taut and pulling
Now loose, curling
floating, drifting

Away from me

I have never known how to let go
So this pain
it burns
soft
and sweet
and slow

Did you feel it too?
I did not think it was just me
but I needed the proof

The knowing
that could stem
and blossom
if we met eye to eye

Our lips would pause
form the same sick words
at the same time

I fear I will never get our closure
The satisfaction
the knowing
this is over

I carry on
to make sense of myself
A scathed and tattered version of me
without you

In this bold new season
I visit with the lake
monthly now

We sit in the silence
my emotions roaring
hers rattling against the shore
Projecting fresh water spray
over my bowed head
Lapping up the remains of our unsettled dust
Carrying the specks of who I once was
far off
to her other shore

I will be different
I tell her
Next time she sees me
I will be changed
wholly and completely
for good

An apology
rips itself from my lungs
sour and burning and strong
I scream
I am sorry
for being the same
the same as last time

I was here

As for now
Today

she breathes me in
a stationary being
full of remorse over fear
Rigid but imaginative
I join her forceful, rhythmic dance

Change takes time
powerful and unforgiving as she is
my lake reminds me

Change takes time
more than I have yet to know
for even she cannot shape her own earth
in a day

My mind casts back far at times
Back to when days felt long
From the first breath of light, sharp morning air
to the last drip of bleeding sun
Hours ran full
of activity or boredom
Dinner always so far in the distance

Back to when money was tight
School lunch was a hope
and a dream
A wide, longing stare
beamed from my eyes at the rec league
cheer team
Girls with clean new tennis shoes
in gym class
Nights of entertainment
contained in the box TV set

Back to when we dreamed deeply
before, during and after sleep at night
Minds rampant with ideas
innovations
invitations
for change

A sheer will and might
the blazing fire of a child who wants
who unwittingly grieves
with just enough force
to believe

Back to times when believing was seeing

Delusion cloaked in imagination
to coast through the mind's gates

My mind casts back
Back to these times
to peer into a young girl's mind

To understand when we decided
to make this real world feel so significant

The shift that turned imagination into just
a light skipping pebble
A figment

Words rumble round in my head
Wet shoes in an old burnt out dryer
never to be said

They tremble in my throat
Dry up on my tongue
Cracked concrete
I once skinned my knees on

Sunk back in my eyelids
Waves stronger than Lake Michigan
pounding on rocks
placed there to break her wake

Her core
too rhythmic to know pause
Her soul
too grand to be halted

She staggers to the shore
Asking for nothing more
than her own forgiveness

7 a.m. is a fine time to wake
The sun seems to think so these days
She will give us a week
to settle in
before she eludes us again

Sneaking up through the morning
Slipping away in the evening
Biting the air with the chill
of her cruel absence

Her disappearance
so monumental
so consequential

The birds will cease warbling
a moment of silence
in a vigil for the return of her light

The night animals will stalk
and howl
The cadence of life
less a worship to her counter force
more a gospel
pleading for her return

It is impossible to predict right now
Someday soon forgiveness will melt over you
in a fashion you have not worn before

A blanket will slip off your shoulders
saturated with the magnitude
unimaginable guilt
for the sacrifices made before you

In a recognition of adult decisions and grief
You will wonder
if your life can ever be the same

Of course it will

The world does not change shape
once you see the weight you hold
in others' lives
An epiphany enveloped
behind your own two eyes

Of course
the earth will not break away at her edges
Decide finally to draw you in
to wrap you in mud
lake water
the heavenly things
we forget make up the land we wander

You can stand
naked and shivering in the bathroom stall
The person you know intimately in your mind
falls to pieces on the floor

But the eyes that meet yours in the mirror
have been here before

Of course
the world does not change
when you actualize your own weight
only your perception of a pound.

Winter

As I grow older
winter chill
begins to fester
in ways anew

I curl my body under the covers
turn over my memories
A new filter cast over each frame

I find I want to apologize
I want to say I am sorry

I am sorry I was not there
to pour you the juice
ask you how you were

But I can't
I cannot be sorry
I did not understand
the weight of an inflating globe
at ten years old

I will not pretend to understand
the secrets you hold
so close to your soul

There is a part of me that wants to
A part of me that knows I never could

I have not cooked a meal
since Babcia passed

She was 97

It was not sudden

We knew it was coming
Still
the grief creeps up on you
Different every time

My grandma just *died*

I saw them put her in the ground
My grandma *just* died

Suddenly
It is winter now
She blinked and took the seasons with her

No time to rake the leaves
It is winter now
but my grandma just died

I will write until my hand cramps
For the sake of preserving something

Anything

One day I will have to remind myself
of this creeping, fleeting feeling
My grandma just died

Yet I stood frozen there
An adult unable to comprehend
how everything feels complicated

None of this is complicated
My grandma just died

I will pick up the pieces
One day I will carry her whole

The cat bathes
in the morning sun
The linear
predictable pattern
of the rays
The last of the grace of the morning
crosses the sofa

Heat disperses
from the floorboards first
Then my coffee
the steam tendrils plucked
from the atmosphere

The sun treks past our window
until the living room sulks hollow
with the chill of the house
to linger for the rest of the day

My little cat looks to me
paws stretch out long
her jaw snaps closed from a yawn
Her back drops down from a lazy stretch
as she trots near to me
seeking warmth from my lap
as I do from her

Something has changed
It is not me
It cannot be
It has to be the weather

The sky grows dark early
Too heavy is the weight of the sun
on the frail shoulders of the clouds

The stars linger
Their gentle sparkle drains heat
from the quiet sidewalks

I break from bed early
Sneaking into the darkness
for a secret, lonesome, glimpse
at the morning sun

A quick shot of redemption
for the day I know lies ahead of me
Simple and plain as the one
I just left behind

This feeling
it cannot be me
It is the weather

In this climate I cannot bear
to shoulder new responsibility
I need to draw away

The curtains can stay open
When there is no light of day

I will lay in bed
Watch the glow fade from the horizon

Tuck myself in deep
while the clock still reads evening
I will sleep the cold away

The cold invites
old parts of me
left unforgotten
untended

The wilted plant
shifts
draws a new root
in a part of me unknown

The cold invites
new parts of me
sharp
unfamiliar edges

My hands shake
to learn where the tender points lie
Fearful of the trip wires
in my own mind

The growth circles
encloses itself around
a stubborn knot
tied by someone once known

Begging an old part of me to wonder
where she will ever find
a light in the darkness

I once desired to live
a plain life
in a mind left completely my own
uninhabited by the push and pull
of forces unknown

I mucked it up early on
Followed curiosity down the rabbit hole
Left myself to toe the line between
positively carefree
and horribly, awfully ashamed
of who I can be

A dabble in the arts
of which I know
are not best for me

But what is left
when I strip away the want
when I long so frivolously

Cobwebs
hang loose
in tight corners

The dirt
dust
lint
tiny specs of life that once were
sit still

Moving only
across the deserted floor
when the wind dares
break through
the cracks in the window pane

The door swings
sudden
but smooth
calculated

Bare feet skim the hardwood
that same dust
sticking awkwardly
to soles
but no longer
will it touch my soul

Tell me
Faint words break through
perpetual silence
A spark in the dark night
while the TV hangs blue with quieting light

Tell me
Am I allowed to appease my selfish parts?
When I have grown tired of it all
When I have no power left to draw

Tell me
Can the stupidity
Can the childishness
of this emerging part of me
be forgiven?

Must there be shame at all,
if she was having fun?

Forgive me
when I wake in the night
longing for your touch

Forgive me
when I beckon
and call to be held

Forgive me
for I was thrust into this world
without the solace of touch
to quiet my tears

Forgive me
in my relentless quest
for quiet, for comfort
in my rolling and roaring mind

Forgive me
for I was once forced alone
into the unknown

Forgive me and understand
I seek only to know
my winds and waters enough
to right my own ship in the storm

Forgive me and know
when I am strong enough to bear my own weight
I will return to you

I will admire the strength
the practice of forgiveness
has carved into you

Frost bites at the windows
when I draw my tired bones from bed
make movement
when the online yoga teacher bids me farewell
She says,
Have an awesome day
Be kind to yourself

Now I will drag myself from the depths
nails wearing thin
Packed beneath with dirt
and distress from days behind
Sickening anticipation
for days ahead

For today
I will embody this to be true
for myself
for that guidance trapped behind a screen

To know
the rain that falls today
will be filled with beauty

Perhaps afterward
I will go for a stroll

It is difficult to admit
when the churn of the day
becomes monotonous
tiring
draining
headache inducing

The stress presses in
without any exceptionally awful
difficult catalyst
It wears you down
before it wears you
as its second skin

The stress you endure
embodies your mind
then your bones
then your soul

Until
you wake in the morning
With no room left to
explore your unknown

Go on a work trip
Stop home
Not the one you have come to know
the one you have known
so long it has become old

Meet your niece
Explore that new piece
of you
of family
A new title to bear with your name

Fly back to your new city
Settle in
to get unsettled again

Jolt to a new idea
to let it fizzle out

Start again
feel renewed

It is strange
belittling
but empowering
to be old enough
these are things we get to do

I yelled at the moon

She did not respond
She gazed down, never asked
My child, what is wrong?

The mother moon knows all
She knows when she is full
her children will call

Fling open their windows
skin nipped dry in bitter December air
They will scream
They will cry
The world is not fair

The mother moon knows all
She need not hear our cries
She knows we use them to stall

She knows
we must only destroy our own guise

She knows
only we have the power
to construct our own calm

There is a piece of me
lost over a sea I have yet to sail
She waits patiently
under my moon
beneath the sky we share

When I bow my head
I plead
I hope
I pray I find her

I beg to learn who she is
A nagging need to know
why she eluded me so long

Press my cheek to the floor
ruminate and frustrate
the tangled thread in my mind

Is she worth the collusion
the derailing
the pain of finding her

Do I wait
until she finally washes up
on my own shore

I know when my alarm buzzes
I will snooze it for a minute

I will get myself up and ready
in the dark of my bathroom
I will know where everything is

I will get dressed
just for the morning
I know I will change at noon

I will go to the gym
my feet will track the treadmill
It will be quiet besides that
I will be alone
everyone but me still

The noise the elevator makes
when it stops at my floor
it will ring in my ears
repeat in my mind
Until my key clicks when it turns in the door

My lover and my cats
will still be warm in bed
when my headphones come gently
off my head

In the kitchen my kettle will whistle
my coffee will brew
ice cubes will hit the glass

All of this will be the same

in each day I take new

I can know all the sounds
hold them close to my chest
take the rest of the day
to figure out the rest

I am afraid
you have nothing left to learn
before you meet her

There are no required preparations
a test to pass
a list to check

She is ready for you
today

Even if your hair lay flat
your palms damp
two tired, too tired
bags rest below your eyes

A breath away from tears
unlike which you have ever known

She knows
She hears
She understands

She is unafraid

The woman you have prepared
your whole life to meet
has always been here

I grapple and strain
with the effort
to hold a moment
the intangible
between my fingertips

Lodge it between the grooves
in my brain
truly remember it

Forever

I run fast
to chase the remembrance
of a feeling

Photos pasted in a book
Receipts stashed in a drawer
Words scribbled on a page
Video recorded on a screen

To rewind
replay
again, again

To feel this now
forever

I battle every emotion
Record every conversation
Catalog the highlights
rip open the lows
Again, again

I will spend forever
searching
pining
For one way way to remember
today
again, again

Forever

To be thankful,
grateful,
is to love your friends
The new and the old

Your friend who invites you out
on a weeknight
to sip tea

Walk the streets
growing now in familiarity
As the sun lays to rest
beyond your train platform

This friend
you have yet to know
she holds her secrets
at arms length
for you
She bears her wingspan
to you
She lets you in

This first friend
in a new city
The first of which you reveal
your new home

Turn the key
cross the threshold
that has yet to know any visitors

To be thankful,

grateful,
is to understand a friend

To know she is not made to replace the old
but to plant new seeds
along a beaten path
foster regrowth
repair the aging soul

It is going to snow tonight
Blanket the city like it should on Christmas
when children are home on break
snow covers their responsibilities
while they lay warm in bed

Morning come
Mom will make pancakes
and bacon

The smell lingers and dances
carefully
wafts its way up the stairs
Gently waking their young senses
A crinkle of the small nose
Eyes drift open only to fall back closed

There is no noise to stir over
for the snow
has silenced all things
that could wake them in full

It is going to snow tonight
but Christmas this year has passed

It is January
I am 23
I will wake tomorrow for work
I hope I will have good rest
I hope the snow will carry in that lulling
drowning effect

It is going to snow tonight

but no sweet aroma will wake me
Maybe the memory alone
will pull me from the covers

It is going to snow tonight
and tomorrow morning
I will make myself pancakes
and bacon

I got drunk with my new friends
Mind numb
Fished my phone from the deep pocket
Thought nothing

Unlock
Scroll
Click

Mindless
until there is a photo of you

Your glass eyes
stare hollow back at me

I realize
we have no memories left

Living now a world apart
An emptiness I never would have believed at the start

Yet I hope
I can wish the best for you
Despite my pride
and entitlement
Bitterness
and shame

I hope neither of us is to blame
for the grand nothing
that left so much pain

I hope your cheeks still freckle

and your smile radiates true

I hope your house smells
like childhood

I hope come Sunday morning
love spills from the oven

I hope each of your animals is hugged
tucked into bed
at the end of the day

I hope that is all it is
I hope we are just tucked away

Inspiration draws a sweltering blaze

A match struck fast against the book
The flame pulls me in
to feel a glimpse of warmth on my face
after long
cold
winter days

No
not too fast now
Hushed
whispered tones rack my mind

The heat will singe my ends
Peel my flesh back to bone

Engulfed in a vast roaring blaze
My mind scatters and writhes to not let go

A slip of the tether
between here and there
is all it takes

This flame dies out
as soon as it smoothers me

It lives anxious
to leave me alone

This list is long
messy
lingering
Not how it feels
How it is

It is January
I hope I feel better tomorrow
but I am doing okay
I have dreams
aspirations
creative energy
that are mine
Mine alone

I got promoted
Learned to care about sports
Decided to call myself an artist
and today I am not angry

It is a Monday
this day,
this week,
this month of the year

I worked hard last week
I want to take my time
I want to rest
It is January

The person I am
The person I was
She who has been depressed
let the cold draw her back under covers
She who has been alone
lost and pining for touch
in the void of her own room

She has dissolved
faded away
reappeared anew
before my own eyes

Today she is home

This home of hers
of mine
It is quiet
It is soft
as it ought to be

The world outside
it rushes by
I am safe to be slow
gentle
tame
inside

Decisions in my own time
I move like ice in the harbor
No need to crash to shore today

A graceful, slow drifting

Rolling over my own mind
in my own time

The world within my fingertips now
If not for the shelter of this very window
leaving only melancholy out of reach

I have not seen her as of late
yet I know
beneath the cold, hard exterior of this soul
there is a part of me
who is most kind

She bubbles
spills over the top
to fill a room with joy

Deeply
relentlessly
she celebrates her friends
cares for her family

Constantly
unapologetically
she wishes the best
for those around her

With her she brings light
A match to ignite
the spirit
the soul
the shine
of others

Somewhere deep within me
I know
She is due to return.

Spring

There will be days all the dishes are dirty
You opened your doors
You let the love and laughter
from your outside world pool in

All the plates will be stained with spaghetti sauce
Your pans crusted with fresh baked bread
Forks holding on to the last bit of frosting
from a cake made with no celebration in mind

There will be days the dishes can sit overnight
because
the glasses are still filled with wine
There is lipstick to be left on the rim

It will still be there tomorrow
when I lift my weary head from the pillow
wondering if you are awake yet
in my living room

Let's go for breakfast
I will declare
because
all my dishes are dirty

It doesn't matter when they get cleaned
if I am spending more time with you

Heat does not always burn bright
With time we learn
there are levels to what we face

There is a heat that engulfs you
mind and essence
skin and bones
on a wicked summer day

Those soon to come near
sun thick and heavy in the sky
you dare to turn away
seek refuge in the shade

There is a heat that allows you
to brace for the cold
Teaches you the patience
resilience
not to flinch
when the wretched winter air
licks at your soul

There is a heat the builds within you
twisted and wicked
in its own right
Singes at your seams
leaves you wondering

You ran from it
you cowered
we know
It is easy
It brings with it fear

Today you kneel softly before it
this heat of your own
invite it to play
Show you what you do
and what you have yet
to know

I long for my Babcia's warmth
Where the hallways lingered
with the scent of dust
dog hair piled up in the corners

Time moved slowly there
for better
or for worse

Every closet drawer held secrets
begging to be told

I was offered coffee
Back then I never accepted
Sprung for a Vernors
in the garage fridge

On a soft evening
the porch swing croaked
a sweet melody

The couch
held space
where Dziadzia once sat

Weeds grew over the garden
but never for long
The kids came along
to pick them
for a treat
Lessons in patience
and empathy

After
we would climb
the tangled branches of the willow tree
I would swear
in the faint dimness of dusk
I could hear fairies

When the day is long and strenuous
I gaze down at my lap
Words tumble and linger in my mind

Double Dutch jump ropes
Skipping stones
Rolling tennis balls
of a simpler time
Unaware of the growing complexity

I am doing just fine
I have to be
how else would I be
where I am

Round and round they come
a whisper
a notice
a promise

I am doing just fine
It is all just fine
As it has been
As it has to be

It rained yesterday
It rained today
It always rains on my birthday

I like it that way

The shower comes
to wash away
those pieces
I did not know
I still carry

I will force a molehill into a home
Tear up the yard
Pack the walls in

Piece by piece
I will tunnel
I will burrow

A pile of things
words
ideas
dirt
it was nothing

Until

Ah
I am alone
No outside noise remains

A space once thought uncomfortable
unwelcoming
Now toasty
Now special
just for me

I will twist
I will howl
No one will hear me scream

Thoughts unsaid
unwritten
rattle through me

Until

Only meek deliverance remains
My thoughts ricochet through the air
escaping toward the hollow spaces
I built

A release
of pang for no one
no thing in particular

Until I emerge
dumbfounded

No one
had heard
a word

When the world grows too sharp
for my tender
soft edges
I hide away
gorge on relics of the past

Cling to a history that could have
may not have
existed

Watery eyes as I gaze down
dream upon
mementos
trinkets
photos
furniture

My own
thrifted
handed down
heirloom
garbage

My inherited need
to fill my pockets
my cabinets
my home
myself
with what I want to know

The simple fragile pieces
to a puzzle of the past
how it brought me up

how it has become an integral
literal
conceptual
physical
part of me

I leave myself predisposed to grief
The daily kind
a broken dish
a finished book
the click
at the end of a phone call

Little acts of finality
intricately designed
to rebel against the nature
of my self preservation
my very being

Simple motions tug at the raw edges
of an ever aching wound
I refuse to let heal
in cautious preparation

A loss undefinable
unimaginable to me
A grief that will finally
tear me at my seams

I live in wicked
unyielding hope
this great grief will recognize me
in my ongoing sacrifice
of leaving myself exposed
A worship
of the pain it has yet to wreak onto me

No one told you
How could they convey
the guttural knowing
learning that brings
heavy realization

There is still Mother's Day

When you are grown
When your mother lives
hundreds of miles away

No one talks about
these days of in between
Balancing roles known and new

On your own
in your city
Not a mother
nor a child

A daughter
an aunt
a girlfriend
independent femininity

Your own state of being
wondering
wandering
through your days of in between

A letter to an ex-best friend:

This one is not about you
Sat down at my desk
posture poised, pen in hand

I ink the month
then check the date

The date
I am notoriously bad at remembering them

Scribble the month, the number
at the top of each page
to hold on to something

But today
this one
will always be for you

A day entirely your own
in my twisted calendar of memory
A promise of your ability to creep in
remind me of when
we ran and rebelled joyously

Just you and me

As warmer times draw near
I am bold enough to admit now
I hit my stride with depression
in May

Call it timely
I earned it
Manifested it
Welcomed it
Sometimes you live to feel that way

Lost my discipline
falling
spinning away

Call it what you want
I caught a wave
flowed through the beige
in May

I have seen the sun
A glint of her light caught on my lash
on my best day

I have touched the rain
before it hits the grass
Breaking the droplets against my skin
bracing for nothing
but the absence of its impact

I have jumped from the dock
Just to make a splash
Dry to my bones
aching for the sharp rushed chill
of a lake I call home

I have been gloriously okay
known blatant content
and airy, wondrous joy

Gentle fingertips on my skin
in the darkest night
and the blinding power
of morning light

The burn of coffee on our tongues
At home
In the woods
In deepest love

As children we were tanned
not because we wanted
or did not want to be

Simply because the world willed for us to be so
By the sheer nature of it all

Sunrises
recesses
baseball games
parks
beaches
backyards
yard work
runs through the sprinkler
ice cream cones on the swings
sunsets

There was no way
to avoid the weathering touch of the sun
to delicate new skin

So we were tanned
not because we wanted to
because there was no other way
Sweet and simple
carefree

The mean streak will become me
if I only let it

Pounding brooding bubbles up
to overflow
breach my defenses
drown those I know

Once I gain my footing
my command over my own will
in the churning, splashing demand of my spite
I will stand tall waiting for the waves to still

Among all I have been before
all I ever will be

The raging emotion deep
rushing to nourish the care
the hope

All of which
I wish to become me

Only within my own bones
Spite, despair
and all
will I become my truth
will I belong

Some days
I exist on a plane
with no success
nor rest

A plane of being
inconsequential doing
Nothing more
nor less

Motivation is low
anticipation is lower

Just here

A twisting
turning over
of the sphere I maneuver

No shake
No strain

A simple
casual
existing within

A slow
knowing preparation
I am ready for what is next

The Earth slowly wakes
dots her fields with wildflowers
The crashing winter waves of the lake calm
to a steady ripple
Life feels light and joyous

Laughs come easy
coaxed out of shallow hiding
by friends who live
to inspire
to love
and be loved

The sun blesses us with
her first welcoming warmth
Her light melting to honey
in my eyes
Begs the question from deep inside
What more could I ask for?

When I am in their company
my sun
my lake
my friends

The light dances on my skin
My soul touches the air

A knowing sweet
kind
tenderness
brushes my deepest self

The Earth
she wakes slowly
welcomes me under her wing
beckoning in another season.

Summer

I reach for the things that make me feel small
Plop me in the city
let the cars and the people rush by
If I can't be the queen
shrink me down to an ant

Insignificant
Most likely to be out of place
least likely to know it in the moment
You won't know it either
for I am only a glance as you run past

Perhaps my struggles
my fears
my worries
will shrink down too
Disperse in the air around me
better my chance at a fresh breath

Once it has escaped
tiny pieces of the world
once mixed and mingled into my blood
my soul
no longer part of my body
belonging to the sheer existence of the world
the next life to take it in

The weight of the world will be different
only a moment away

The world turns new leaves
A child grows into her own
Lessons once old
are new again

In this wild, winding new life
the words from a teacher creep in
at a critical time

Echoing through me
ricocheting from my core

Some whispering, begging part of me
never left the room
where they were spoken

Tacked to the wall
recited
in an oath
to no one but myself

Writers write
a lot

As dancers dance
a lot

Or bakers bake
a lot

This writing
this never ending practice
It is not to be good

It is to feel something

The feeling
need not be new
or novel

All it must be is present
and true

It can be clear
or cluttered

So long as it is here
it is mine
to write
to share

I feel Great Grandma in the lake breeze
when I step outside
She was happy here once
as I am now

Her lingering presence
blends softly
in the contour of my own existence
A gentle mingle of her own memory
and fierce, present emotion
wrap loose around my fogged mind

Today
Tomorrow
Yesterday
We watch the boats maneuver to the bay
Let the sun kiss our cheeks
a sweet loved one
returning home from the long voyage
of winter

Someday I will tend tomato plants
as Great Grandma did once
I will hoard my secrets deep
in my chest
as trinkets to her pockets
and cabinets
and drawers
Relying on only myself
to recall their truth in their hiding places

Until one day when I burst at the seams
As her fridge overflowed

preserves and cookies
I will let my lips loose
wild memories
of summer days and road trips
Dogs once known and babies held tight
Friends forever to be treasured

Today the wind has lost its chill
Sweat beads across my crinkled brow
Still I hold fast
to Great Grandma's stiff denim jacket
patched with memories

I plead to the sky
one day it will teach me to live and love
as Great Grandma did once

All grandmas drink coffee
Least
in my world they do

Babcia, Gerp, Great Grandma, Grandma Bloom
Their favorite mugs are faded and worn
The pot always ready to brew

At a moment's notice
On the deck
in the den
around the table
Half-caf
decaf
With cream
with sugar
Before breakfast
after dinner
Anytime

On Christmas Day
at 22
I offered Great Grandma coffee
Mom pulled down mugs we rarely use
Decked with floral patterns
and frills
a saucer to match

Poured from the aging pot
softened with milk
I topped it with whipped cream
How rich
What a treat

She told me

Great Grandma cracked a smile
wide enough to still the room
halt my soul

Her eye glistened
bright enough for me to lean forward
listen closer

Coffee
for grandma
is commonplace

No bells or whistles
No frills

I knew then as I do now
the treat of it
is found not within its creation
or flavor

No
the treat of it
is the time spent waiting for the beans to steep
and brew
with the people sat around the table

It is not Christmas
The decorations have long been put away
Scents of fir and sugar cookies
no longer linger

When I close my eyes
I am still there
passing a mug across the counter
a welcome chill bites the air

I wake to the fan
roaring in the corner
Sun hot
across the floor boards
The hollow in my chest
actualized by the pleading
repetitive thought
There is no playbook for death

You will deal
You will deal again

I rack my brain
seeking, hoping, searching
wishing there was more to it

I come up short
I am not sure anyone knows
if it will ever end

There is a part of me that carries on
despite knowing exactly what is wrong

She wakes for a morning workout
Energizes her bones for a coffee
Smiles for the man on the bench
outside her favorite coffee shop
The baristas play her favorite song
a knowing nod from the universe

She will be okay

She walks to the lake
Writes mediocre poetry
Calls her mom
Reminds herself to keep her patience
with my friends
and my family
and strangers

She is changing
She will be okay

She carries envy and anger
She is learning where it came from
and how it can exist beside pure joy and calm

She is okay

There was a time
I spoke with such conviction
no one stopped to question
what I thought
where I went

Full speed to the finish line
or spinning out of control
Only supernatural
curious forces
possessed the ability
to call me to a halt

No one who knows me
my mind
and heart
and soul
has the power
to question my will
or my way

How curious
those who know nothing
are the only beings
to make a question of who I am
what I am capable of

How devastating
the moments in which
I chose to listen

Now the deep summer has set in
Rusted metal on wheeled carts
bare the weight of wooden flower boxes

Longer than they are wide
slapped with thick green paint
revealing deep grain
running horizontal across the planks

The boxes spring forth with wild flowers
varying size
differing hue

Deep magenta coneflower
Rich yellow, orange gold baby daisies
Wispy light forget-me-nots

A long green stem
pokes over the highest flowers
Simple greenery some might call a weed
Sucks, reflects
the green of the box it sprouts from

It stretches and bends
to offer the bumble bee
the humble pollinator
a place to rest

He scouts his pallet below
for the sweet nectar
that will bring him home

The tiny fuzzy insect

holds fast
but light
to his vibrant target

Careful
purposeful
He takes what he needs
leaves what he does not

Does he know
the flowers
exist for him
because of him

No

The tiny bee lives blissfully unaware
he foots the burden to create the flower
He believes
he exists to eat and feed his own

This flourishment of others
a glimmering
miraculous side effect
of existing
for the maintenance of his own existence

The flowers have bloomed
new again
Young chickadees bathe in the dry dust
preserved under leaves and vines
Different cars park
along the same street
I walk carefully
deliberately each morning

Somewhere between the thrill of new life
the excitement of beginnings
a cloak of aching familiarity
draped itself around my quiet corners

In the wild, chill breeze of
achievement of dreams
I wonder
if destiny exists at all

What am I left to owe
but a life felt worth living

A soul worn tired from reckless believing

A dream all the while
worth keeping

I keep my suitcase
out all summer
I make the plans
have places to be
Give anything to be
anywhere but here
everything but still

I wake tired
a devoted craving
to the feeling of the earth
spinning fast beneath my feet
To remind myself
my own movement is nothing
compared to her entirety

I feed the desire to dive deep
into the sea that scares me
A perpetual drive to experience new
hold it all close

The full and comprehensive expansion
of who I can be
peeks desperately around
the next corner

She must not be far off
but she is not here
I must be anywhere but here

It is a new age phenomena
to feel inadequate in work
in life

An impostor deployed to play the part
of a willing observer
a careful participant
in your own day to day

Do not fear
for the day will come
when the city you have dreamed of
rushes by your windows
Work you aspired to
fills your desk

One morning
the Earth shifts
now your core sits
at an unsettling 45 degrees
upright in your own mind

You are cut out for
this life you lead
but the ache
and the twist
is not all it was chalked up to be

I live to drop the things
I worked hard to carry

Built comfort into my life
only to discover
a priority
to destroy it

The values I once drew close
gripped tight to my chest
draped over my shoulders

Brought comfort only until
they grew heavy
My body grew dreary

I set them down
step away
My feet draw up roots from the ground
as I run fast past what I know
to see what is left
what has grown to stay

I might relish
in the struggle
in the fight
The exercise to recognize
my own right in the life I lead

I let myself throw a fit
feel anything I need to feel
the unparalleled joy and grief
of unknowing

It will not be long
until I find more to carry
the day I wake up
to begin another story

There are only so many things
you let define you

When your candle is lit
has melted down the mantel
gone out at both ends

When fury rides up
pure emotion cannot be reeled in

When the weight of every unconscious decision
pulls you down to the floor

There are only so many things
you let define you
Will this be one of them?

Tomorrow
the clouds will roll by
sunlight will seep in

A quiet morning alone
together
in bed

Your coffee
freshly brewed
cooled just right

Your book
awaiting the turn of a page
forgiving of that coffee
that may leave a stain

Your cat
curling in your lap
purring a sweet song that sounds like your name

A still mind
simple curious delight

There are only so many things
you let define you
Let this be one of them.

I fear if I do not write it down
I will forget
the moments of this life
which bring me the most happiness

I worry my voice will fall lost
in a sea of other noises
eclipsed and silenced
within my own busy mind

Perhaps I will forget
what I had for breakfast this morning
If I ran or if I walked
Where the cats snuggled in
when I fell asleep last night
If my coffee was cold or hot

The supreme and joyous mundane
lives in a fleeting state
I am not accustomed to

I pine for a page
I beg and I pray

But I will not forget
My hair welcomes a cool breeze
My toes, the sand on the beach
My arms beg to stretch wide
My lungs long to sing
My eyes search for the stars
My heart is to be free

If I could visit
who I once was
a month
a year
ten years
ago

I would tell her:
The still of the world
can be boring
It will not kill you

You can still too
Take in the monotony around you
as stagnant as it feels
the days and weeks blur together
in a blinding haze

It will never feel this way again

Do what makes your heart jump
Give, just a little more
than you think you can

You are doing just fine
you will continue to
until the end of our time

Unknown lingers
quiet and constant
Uninvited visitor to daily life
unnoticed and untouched
until

I wake in the morning
unsure if it will rain
or shine

A stark remembrance
brief resemblance we live
unsure if we will live
or die

There are signs
cues
The clouds roll in
Leaves flip to bare
viny underbellies

Will there be signs?
Will the world slow and blur
before the lights run out,
before our tears run dry?

Nothing to run from
the impending, looming sky

Somehow we remain content
In this constant
uneasy unknowing
Live to fret

to sweat
the minor casualties of the day

Now it is raining
I should have checked the weather

The words
I once pondered the meaning of
now slip naturally
in conversation

A recent discovered river
of nonchalance
flowing freely
from work and practice and play
to find home
lodged between my brain
and my lungs inhaling to push them out

No one explained
Did not sit me down
lay it out
Spelling
Definition
Example

One day it arrived
a knowledge
barren
if not for the repetition of existence
Meaningless
if not for the hunger to find meaning

To live
is to miss
to be missed

The bus
The invitation
The phone call

A decision
a choice to go
to experience
to grow

Leading only to
a passing of some other experience
never to be reclaimed

Still we wonder
What if something had changed
Where would we be
Where would we go

If we knew what we missed
If we let go

Despite careful consideration
calculation to an unfathomable degree
desired precision and perfection
deliberate execution

I still drag my heart
down trails untraveled
Once purposefully forgotten
folded neatly and cast aside

Now a weed covered garden
full of contorted
twisted abandon

My foot slips
ankle twists
between mangled root
and scarce solid ground

Spider webs
whip around my head
branches across my face
as hands rush fast to the ground

The moment skips
instead of wreckage and debris
of who I once was
who I ought to be

My palms crash deep
a chilling dive
into a still pool
Remnants of the past

suspended in crystal clarity

A delicate tumble
urging a careful
deliberate reconsideration
rediscovery of what was once
left unsaid

How curious
the living paradox

Waking
breathing every day
for the self
for you

An innate impulse
destined to battle
the want to cower
to hide
when revealed to you
is your own desire

Why banish your thinking mind
Cast away into the shadows
you have yet to explore
by the whims of your shallow thirst
to live for a moment
over a lifetime

I can imagine living nowhere
but beside the shore
My lake
my beauty
this is all for you

The mother of all
known and unknowing
If I lived for nothing
I would be at peace
to serve you

Glorious lake
I know not where any other desire
passion
of mine originates
but from you

Dearest Lake Michigan
my gratitude resides in my soul
The wholeness of my being
I belong to nothing
if not to you

I know
one day
you will take me in
I will sip
but you will swallow me whole

I plead to my soul:
When I speak
let it be from my heart
let my words ring true
to the largest part
of my being

Let my words be cautious
when I say:
My legs beg to run
My arms wake to stretch
My fingers curl to grasp
the dreams my mind stills to create

My heart beats to love
My ears perk to listen

Let my lips part
to speak kindness
sturdy truth

Is there nothing else we can wish for
but the declaration of who we are
The desires of our heart

In youth I stood tall with
a resilience of childhood
Towering stone fortress
built brick by brick
of wondrous curiosity and innocence
surrounded me on every side

Part of me believes
I was stronger then
or I am softer now

A palace that saved me
from cringing at the bitter wind of this life
as I poked my head out of this
my highest turret

Now day in and day out
the stones erode beneath me
beaten back by the shock
disbelief
from encountering what lies beyond my walls

In this sense
I am softer now
yet I can still push my weight from the ground
to believe
strength and weakness
as they are
may need not be
mutually exclusive

To grow is to recognize
discomfort is not synonymous with discontent

Discomfort sits
an idle prerequisite to the unknown
A necessary hurdle to our next best

Discontent nestles and brews
Wraps a heavy blanket over you
She will whisper in your ear
You cannot shake her

Discontent will linger
She snickers
presses down on your head
with long pointed fingers
Offers you bargains
Makes you plead

When you stand in the mirror
face to face with the girl
you know best
Ask her

Which of these ghosts is with me
How much farther must I trek
Before I can look them in the face
Before I can ask them to rest

A declaration

In contrast to
a long believed and
enforced misconception
I know it now to be true

I am not a mean person

There may not even be a mean part of me
though I have not completed the examination
not yet

Please
strike the word
from the list used to define me

The adjective does not fit
the sentiment
I leave in my wake

I take myself
seriously

That does not mean
I emit
the sharp
deliberate
cruel and calculated
opposite
of kindness

I believe in myself

wildly

By simple definition
I am true
to myself
through every part
that shines through

I can wind myself
so tightly within my own head

When an imminent
crucial escape lies
just beyond my door

As I took to the lake
I knew I would find you here

The peace
reverberating stillness
which escapes me in my mind
my home

The gentle known that comes
from unlocking
removing my mind
from its imagined boundaries

Mental scissors
clip the wings
of the wild belief flying within

Not here
The power
Knowingness of self
As it were
As it is

I knew I would find you here
The piece of me
buried so deep inside

She resides
not in my soul but
within your deep
vast knowing

A year ago
I did not know the difficulty
of keeping this room clean

I dusted up the corners
swept up the floors
drew back the curtains
sparkling sunlight bounced off the white walls
heated the wood floors

I clasped my hands before me
declared I would keep my quiet routine
forevermore

Then I spilled my coffee in a rush
The cat scratched up the couch
Our friend stained the sheets
We knocked wine on the carpet
Soiled the table cloth
Littered the floor with crafts and artifacts

Now dust settles in corners
I have never seen before

There was a time
I did not know we could struggle
to keep the walls white
ourselves still
our minds calm

The world pleads with chaos
and mess
does not ask

before disturbing your happiness

I look around
a space
still mine
perhaps more now than ever before

I see now
we would be remiss
to keep these walls white
with loneliness.

ACKNOWLEDGMENTS

Thank you, reader, for spending your time with me. Thank you for allowing me to share my words, my thoughts, my feelings with you. I myself am an incredibly slow reader and understand the meticulous and careful task of picking your next read. If this was your first book this year or your twentieth, I thank you for opening it and for sharing precious moments with me.

Thank you to the friends and family who stood by and offered a helping hand while I poured myself into this work, my first book. I always wanted to write a book. I wanted to do it for myself, but along the way I began to do it for you, with you. Thank you to my best friend and boyfriend, Dylan Kiefling, for allowing me to lock myself away nights and weekends while I found the words to string this piece together. Thank you for your patience and understanding as we navigate change after change. As we explore each unknown together. Thank you to my closest friends turned diligent editors Daisy Dow, Luke Kaelin and Tiana Petricevic. In moments where I thought this project had turned to a dead end, I thought of your encouragement and devotion to helping me create this art. Thank you to my sister,

Alison Buffin, for being my final beta reader and for reassuring me that this is "a real, full-fledged book."

Thank you to my many other friends and family. Those of the past, present, and future, who inspired words between these pages. The person I am today would not exist without you and the incredible amounts of love and friendship I have been afforded from you over the years.

Lastly, thank you to the small businesses, coffee shops, and bookstores of Chicago for opening your doors. I spent much of my time over the past two years hunkered down over my laptop in Chicago's cafes writing, rewriting, and editing these very words. I am full of gratitude for the lively and welcoming neighborhoods in this city.

You can read me again
front to back
back to front
but you are different now
maybe you will find
I have changed too.

www.ingramcontent.com/pod-product-compliance
Lightning Source LLC
Chambersburg PA
CBHW031423120626
46545CB00006B/2250